The New American Anthem

Jeremy Lloyd Griffith

DEDICATION

I dedicate this text to libertarian heroes Ayn Rand and Andrew Breitbart, and to my lovely wife Roselle Taburada who always inspires me!

CONTENTS

ACKNOWLEDGMENTS

I want to acknowledge my many mentors in the Full Sail University New Media Journalism masters program. You gave me the tools to pursue great citizen journalism. I am forever in your debt.

1 INTRODUCTION

This book is not about changing the National Anthem of the United States, rather it is about either keeping the nation as it was founded, improving the bits that require improvement, or fundamentally trying to recreate a nation based on a totally different system. This is the "Fundamental Transformation" that Barack Obama spoke about when he was president of the United States.

Here is a little background to clarify things for the reader. I started the American Millennium Online blog as a school project for my masters in New Media Journalism at Full Sail University in January of 2012 and have been adding articles to it ever since. Since graduation in 2013, I've been blogging intermittently ever since. I created the blog in hopes of collecting and crafting stories that I thought demonstrated the goodness of the American Republic. In order to preserve some of them, I've decided to include them in a full-sized book, so that they wouldn't just disappear if the blog were suddenly to go down. This is the premise for this work.

Ensuring American Greatness for the next Millennium and beyond was the mantra that I chose to center all of this work upon. But there is another mantra that is shorter, easier to remember, and much more popular: Make America Great Again. This of course is the mantra of the first term of the Donald J. Trump presidential campaign.

These two philosophies, Fundamental Transformation vs. MAGA are the philosophies that are competing for dominance at the time of this writing. Whether or not the country survives as the Republic as founded or if the progressive movement is able to create the socialist utopia they so desperately seek is in question. Each movement is attempting to erase the other. Our political life has never been so volatile.

In 1937, the Libertarian poet Ayn Rand wrote a short novella entitled Anthem. This was to precede her greater works such as Atlas Shrugged and the Fountainhead. In Anthem the main protagonist, Equality 7-2521, is living in a dystopian society where all individuality is crushed and all emphasis is placed on the collectivist state. This society is successful in dominating the culture and erasing individualism, until Equality 7-2521 rebels. He finds an underground railway system and hides there with a friend, conducting scientific experiments and reading books. When discovered, he flees with his lover to the woods to establish a new life and society. I often feel like this lonely man, reading books in my basement apartment and writing controversial political blogs to broadcast to one or two of my loyal readers. I think a lot of people would like me to shut my mouth and go away.

The title of the book then is a nod to the visionary work of Ayn Rand who in 1937 had the vision to see what was happening and rebelled against it. Her work inspired millions and her impact is still alive today.

Another visionary motivated me to write, and I met him briefly in 2011 at a conservative/libertarian blogging conference in Minneapolis, RightOnline. Back then Andrew Breitbart was larger than life and a big thorn in the side of the leftist utopians. I remember seeing him strolling nonchalantly from the conservative conference to the leftist blogging conference across the street, Netroots Nation. The leftists over there hounded him relentlessly, practically spitting insults in his face. He just ignored them and walked through. This was at the time that the photos of Anthony Weiner's junk were floating around and everyone was mad that this libertarian messiah was exposing their favorite pervert to scorn and public ridicule. I remember one blogger shouting the most off the wall questions at Andrew, like: tell us about your first homosexual encounter, or, what is your illegal drug of choice, cocaine or marijuana? Just ridiculous stuff. Andrew just walked through the crowds and ignored them, allowing them to self-implode in their unbridled hatred. It was something to see. Of course, we lost him the following year, but his legacy lives on. Each day I try to write stories that influence and motivate, the way that he did.

At the time of this writing, leftist controlled media of course in continuing to try to erase all conservative or libertarian thought that hits the public square. Facebook and Twitter will ban you, demonetize you our put you in Facebook jail. Their excuse is inappropriate content that doesn't meet their nebulous decency guidelines, but really, it's because right is right, and they can't compete with the uncomfortable truths that they are confronted with. Rather than debate and add legitimacy, they just erase you. This is happening to so many people, like Mark Dice, Alex Jones, and even James Woods. I think they'd like to delete Trump's Twitter account, but they don't know how to deal with the backlash of presidential power.

At the time of this writing, Brett Kavanaugh has been appointed to the Supreme Court of the United States as an associate justice confirmed by the senate. The leftist loons are losing their minds, pounding on the doors of the SCOTUS building, doors without handles. They tried to smear him as a rapist and a drunk but when that didn't work, so they went back to their normal insane meltdowns and self-pity parties. In Rochester, Minnesota where I'm from, a reporter for a local TV station was fired for wearing a MAGA hat at a Trump rally. That's what happens to you when you step out of line. The left erases you. A tough lesson for a young journalist who made a minor mistake in his professional life.

They'd like to erase us all, and so I've tried to branch out in other media adventures in order to get my work out into the public square and keep it there. This then is an example of that. Don't think that you can read this book like a normal book, although you could. You can skip around by topic and not miss a thing. This is a collection of some of my favorite blogs throughout the years. I hope you are inspired by these and I hope that you will be seeing more of them in the near future.

Regards,
Jeremy Griffith, creator of The American Millennium Online blog

A girl in a fancy blue dress competes at the fair as younger girls watch in awe. -photo by Jeremy Griffith

2 STEALING JOY

I know a girl who loves horses. It's fair season and she's not competing in any of the events. That's because toxic people have stolen her joy.

This girl, we'll call her Emily, loves to ride her Arabian horse, Joker! Over the years since she was a little girl, they've created a special bond. Until recently, Emily enjoyed showing in the different events at the Olmsted County Fair, and at other events. Her favorite was her participation in a show team, where a bunch of girls performed as a group, doing special moves in synchronization. Think of it as a dance squad for horse and rider. She worked hard and earned a leadership position, she was given the lead, and a whistle, to signal to the other riders the next move to be performed. She was at the top of her game, and her happiness!

But other people couldn't leave things alone. It wasn't other girls and their jealous ambitions that unseated her. It was the parents of the other girls, a few parents in particular. You see, certain parents couldn't stand the fact that their child wasn't the lead, wasn't the star. And through toxic jealousy and bullying, they drove Emily out of her slot and out of the club altogether. Stunned into submission, the young girl I know left the club and her friends and now sits at home in a blue funk of depression. Her tears are hidden, even swallowed. Her joy is stolen.

This kind of thing happens more than you realize. Bullying by another child is bad enough. But bullying by an adult towards a child is unacceptable. It should be stomped out and burned with fire, like a spider in a house. It is vile and toxic and should have no place in any sport. Performing in front of a crowd with your horse can be pure joy, but there is a dark side to the fair!

Children have dreams, and nothing inspires dreams for a girl than an older girl performing with her horse in front of a crowd. The applause arises from the stands and the adulation is infectious. It's pure joy. I went to the Olmsted County Fair today and took a few shots of the competitors. Along the railing, young people gathered and watched in awe as the older girls performed. It was magic. As much as I enjoyed that moment, all I could think of is that girl I know sitting at home, disappointed that the sport she loved no longer brings her joy.

I have a message for toxic parents. It's not about you and your child. You don't have to kill the dreams of other kids to elevate your own. You are worse than a thief. You are a murderer. You kill dreams.

If you are a parent who participates in the fair, whatever the event, be on the lookout for toxic people and stand up to them. Protect the dreams of all the kids. There is enough happiness and pride for all. Toxic people suck the air out of the room. They should be rooted out and asked to step aside. They don't belong.

I took a few shots of exhibitors today at the fair. I was impressed by their performances. Whoever wins, I hope they all had a good time, ignorant of any toxicity that may lurk at the fair. The older ones inspire the younger ones, who hope to grow up like them someday. Remember parents and competitors. There is nothing wrong with a white ribbon. The white shows that you participated, and hopefully learned something. The red ribbon says you did better this time and you are learning, but still have room to grow. The blue means you are getting really good and your hard work is paying off. The violet and the purple of Reserve Grand Champion and Grand Champion means that you are at the top of your game. Congratulations. Use your status to teach and inspire other competitors and share your love of the game.

And parents, remember, you can't buy your child's happiness by trying to destroy the happiness of others. There is no place for that kind of vile toxicity at the fair!

3 COWARDS OF THE COUNTY

Normally, I'm a very pro-law enforcement guy, which makes this column all the more painful to write. It has been reported that in addition to the school resource officer failing to go into the Florida school to stop the horrible massacre, his buddies, three of them, also failed to do their jobs and enter the school.

Now, from a tactical point of view, I can see why sheriff's deputies did this. Rushing headlong into a potential ambush is not a fun time. But when you are charged with protecting your community and your neighborhoods, especially young people, that is your job! You are the sheepdog protecting the sheep. You have to go, and if you can't go, you shouldn't be in that line of work.

It appears that the school resource officer, Scot Peterson, who was on campus at the Florida school when the gunfire was sounding throughout his campus, took a position of safety and let four precious minutes tick by while people were dying inside. Likewise, his compatriots also took position outside and occupied a wait-and-see attitude while students, teachers and staff were being slaughtered.

What is particularly brutal about the whole thing is, that the Broward County Sheriff Scott Israel attended a CNN sponsored townhall the other day and used that platform to blast the NRA and it's millions of Law-Abiding members, when he knew, HE KNEW, that his department failed to act in defense of children! Wow.

I think there should be an outside investigation into all the failures of this department, what I will now call the Broward Cowards, and that Scott Israel should resign his post as sheriff. Get someone in that position who really shows initiative in protecting the citizens he is charged with defending, not someone just interested in a big fat paycheck.

Some people decry the militarization of the police force. I am not one of them. Buy them the MRAP armored vehicle. Put Kevlar helmets and body armor in every vehicle, right next to the defibrillator and first aid kit, put an AR-15 or M4 rifle in every squad car, right next to the shotgun. And for the love of our children, train these officers to run towards the danger and not away from it.

Nobody wants to see a police officer shot in the line of duty. Our hearts break when we hear that has happened. Our hearts are broken now, for all those kids and teachers, and their respective families. If this horrible shooting has shown us anything is that the government with its huge budget and all its assets is still not sufficient to protect us. Ultimately we are responsible for protecting ourselves. Go get some training, jiu-jitsu, tae kwon do, judo; get a gun and become proficient at shooting; join the NRA and get some professional training. I am a member, and I am proud of it. At the end of the day, I love cops, I support them, but I realize that I am solely responsible for the defense of myself and my family. I have to be the sheepdog because I can't depend on anyone else to do it. That's why I have an AR-15, and other guns. If someone tries to harm me or my family, the cops can clean up the mess when they get there, because it's going to be over very quickly.

I fully agree with some of what has been said about mental health in this country and how it has been neglected. Institutions should be brought back to attempt to help the mentally ill and treat those who have long-term problems. They should be heavily regulated and monitored so the rights of those receiving treatments are being protected and these institutions do not denigrate into the cesspools they once were. There should be outpatient programs so that people battling this disease can graduate to a level of normalcy within their communities, under the supervision of trained mental health staff. And, for the violently insane, there should be a legal process to strip them of their rights to own a gun and a way for their names to be added to the no-buy list.

All of these safeguards, we know, can fail. Every one of the safeguards put in place in Florida failed. Banning guns, even certain kinds of guns, will not help. Famed Texas sniper Charles Whitman used a deer rifle with a three-round box magazine to commit his crimes. Evil will find a way. But the law-abiding should not be blamed for the actions of a few insane villains.

For further reading:

http://abcnews.go.com/US/florida-sheriff-investigating-deputies-remained-school-shooting/story?id=53325711

https://www.cnn.com/videos/politics/2018/02/22/gun-town-hall-full-version-parkland.cnn

http://dailycaller.com/2018/02/22/cnn-town-hall-planted-question-gun-control/

4 DARKNESS DAVE

The microphone pops and fizzes ever so briefly as the circuit opens, then the creepy theme music starts, followed by the booming, confident baritone of Dave Schrader as he introduces the beginning of his radio show, "Darkness Radio" a show about the paranormal and unexplained.

"GOOD EVENING AND WELCOME! You're tuned in to the best in paranormal talk radio, Darkness Radio is on the air!" exclaims Schrader over the airwaves. "I'm you're host Dave Schrader along with your co-host Mallie Fox and producer Tim Dennis. Good evening kids."

"Good evening," Fox's melodic voice cuts in.

"Howdy," says Dennis, simply.

Schrader, 44, of Minneapolis, is at home behind the microphone and plays the part of an 11 to midnight talk radio show host: congenial , professional and inquisitive. If you met him on the street at that hour you might be nervously impressed. Dressed in black leather racing jacket, jeans and skulls T-shirt, his tall, broad-shouldered form is imposing, appearing more like an outlaw biker than a talk show host. His shiny bald head and touch-of-gray goatee are distinctive.

But in the studio, nobody can see him but in-studio guests and co-workers, and on the air, only his voice can be heard which is professional and reassuring. That's good because the topics discussed on the show can be disturbing: ghosts, alien abductions, hauntings, strange creatures, UFOs, etc.

Fox sits to Dave's right at the round table there in the studio, her appearance and demeanor are in stark contrast to that of her co-host. She is sprite and bubbly, with her canary yellow windbreaker and her bleach blonde hair, she stands out in a crowd. She fiddles with a rhinestone encrusted smart phone and adds color commentary when needed through the microphone in front of her. Dennis sits in the glassed-off booth behind her in front of an enormous and complicated radio show producer's control panel where he manages the show, including the phone lines for listeners and guests. His dress is simple: shorts and a Nietzche themed black T-shirt with the scrolling phrase, "What doesn't kill me only makes me stronger".

Genesis of a Radio Program

The trio have been working together on the show for three and a half years at their present home, Twin Cities News Talk, a conservative news and commentary station in Minneapolis, Minnesota. Before that, Schrader and Dennis have been together for over seven years, ever since Dennis, a radio producer at the time, asked his college friend to return to radio. The two men had been attending Winona State University and had done college radio together, Schrader said. Dennis remained in radio and Schrader went on to other things, he said.

"It was about seven and a half years ago when Tim was working for a station," Schrader recalls. "They were looking for a new talent to fill in a time slot and he asked me what kind of show I wanted to do. I told him, 'let's do a paranormal show! That'll be different!'"

So the show was launched at local station KLBB AM in Minnesota and for the next few years bounced around from station to station until they found their current home three years ago. In the intervening years, the format and timing of the show has changed, but the theme has remained the same. Fox got involved three years ago through a mutual friend and joined the team. On this particular evening they are interviewing Rosemary Ellen Guiley, a paranormal researcher with 45 books on the paranormal to her credit. The current book, "The Vengeful Djinn" is tonight's topic, as Dave and company delve into the mystery of the jinnis of Medieval Arabic lore and current philosophy on the subject with the guest.

Dave as story teller

Schrader's experience with the unexplained didn't begin with the show, it followed him all his life, even from his earliest days. As he puts it, "I didn't get involved in the paranormal, it got involved with me."

Schrader recalls stories from his parents on how as a child of three-years old, he would have conversations with his recently deceased grandmother in their old house. It seemed to be more than just a child's fantasy, Schrader explained, since he was able to give a description of his grandmother's burial outfit, down to the fact that they had removed her false teeth. The funeral had been closed casket and only a few people knew the details, impossible to know for a child of three, Schrader said.

"I don't remember being creeped out by the experience," Schrader said. "I loved my grandparents and had a good relationship with them. I just put this experience in the area of the strange."

Schrader's mom related the story to an aunt, who also had unexplained experience with the grandmother, and was disturbed and intrigued by Schrader's accurate, detailed descriptions.

"My grandmother called my aunt on three occasions after she died," Schrader said. He didn't elaborate.

The scary experiences would come later. Schrader describes an event that happened to him when he was living in Illinois at the age of 12.

"I was walking past a house in the neighborhood," Schrader explained. "Back then we didn't have cable and people wouldn't watch TV all day, they would stand in front of their picture windows and watch the neighborhood."

That's what seemed to be happening when Schrader was walking home one day and past a particular house. A man was seen there in front of the window watching Schrader as he passed by. That wasn't so odd. What was odd is when Schrader looked back a moment later, the man was no longer in the window, he was outside on the lawn. A third look and the man was nearly to the sidewalk following Schrader.

"Nobody can move that fast," Schrader said, his voice and mannerisms becoming more excited as he related the story. "In the blink of an eye this person had moved from behind the window, to the middle of a lawn, through a thick hedge and nearly to the sidewalk. I can't explain what I saw."

There was no sign or sound of the front door opening, no footsteps, only a man, who appeared never to move, appearing suddenly closer and closer as Schrader passed by.

"The third time I saw him I just turned and ran the rest of the way home, there was no turning back then," Schrader said. "To this day when I go to my parents' house, I take the long way so I can avoid that creepy house."

Now at age 44, Schrader takes his experience in the paranormal to a whole new level as he leads investigations of the unexplained throughout Minnesota and beyond. He and his cohorts investigate hauntings, and host conferences on the paranormal called "Darkness Events" where he invites experts to speak to fans of the paranormal.

Author and TV Personality

Schrader is the co-author of a book for teens called, "The Other Side: A Teen's Guide to Ghost Hunting and the Paranormal" with co-authors

Marley Gibson and Patrick Burns. The trio hammered out the book in an afternoon coffee shop session, back in 2009, Schrader said.

Schrader has branched out into TV as well, appearing as a celebrity judge for the Travel Channel's show "Paranormal Challenge" last year. Schrader filmed 12 episode where he and other paranormal experts judged competing amateur ghost hunting teams as they jointly investigated haunted settings. His friend Zak Bagans, host of "Ghost Adventures" TV program on the Travel Channel asked him to join the team and bring his healthy skepticism to the show, Schrader said.

"That's what I've always tried to bring to the my listeners and viewers, a sense of the real," said Schrader. "I'm a skeptic and a believer, a little bit of both."

There are no plans now to do more episodes of "Paranormal Challenge" but if asked, Schrader is open to the opportunity he said. Right now though he is focused on making his radio show the best it can be and expanding it from one hour five nights a week to two or three hours a night. Now the show can be heard on Twin Cities New Talk 1130 AM from 11 to midnight. "Darkness Dave" and company can be found on Twitter and Facebook as well as their regular website darknessradio.com.

Though the show isn't syndicated, many make the mistake that it is, due to the fact that Internet podcasts and live streaming audio reaches a far greater audience than the "terrestrial" radio station does, Schrader said.

"We have listeners all over the country and in Europe as well," Schrader explained. "The audience is huge and it is so large because of the benefits of the Internet. Many can't believe it when we tell them we are not a syndicated show."

Things were not always such smooth sailing for the show, Schrader admits. A short time ago management changed at the station, as well as a transition from FM back to AM that shook things up a bit. A new executive called the paranormal host into the office for a meeting, Schrader recalled.

"The guy said basically, 'what are you doing on my station? Justify your existence!'" recalled Schrader. To the executive, a show on the paranormal didn't seem to be a good fit on a conservative talk radio station, apparently. "We went over the (Arbitron) ratings and I basically demonstrated that we were higher rated and kept listeners longer in our hour than many syndicated shows at that time!"

The executive understood and that was that, Schrader said.

The Darkness Radio team chalks up the success of the program to the commitment of the fans and the diversity of ways the audience can listen and participate. Schrader books most of the guests and tries to keep it fresh. Dennis manages the show through technology and Fox adds a fresh perspective to the listeners. Podcasts can be found at twincitiesnewstalk.com.

5 ENEMY OF THE PEOPLE

We know the leftist media is biased, but are they blind? That is a question I asked myself again when I attended a play this weekend on my 47th Birthday this past Sunday. My parents took my wife and I to see a Chanhassen production of Newsies.

Chanhassen Dinner theater is a nice little venue in the City of Chanhassen in the Twin Cities. We've gone there many times. My mom Kathy loves the theater and even prodded my brother and I to take part in local theater productions when we were kids. More about the Disney play Newsies in a moment.

But I want to talk about what happened before the play. I was reading a playbill for another theater company in the Twin Cities, the Guthrie, putting on a production called Enemy of the People. We arrived at the play early and as we waited to be seated for dinner, my mom asked me to grab a pile of the pamphlets to see what else was playing. I grabbed a handful of them and handed half of them to mom while I read the others. I came upon the Guthrie playbill containing the ad for Enemy of the People. Curious, I Googled the play on my smart phone, and I was shocked at what I found.

A New York Times article no less popped up on my phone and hailed the return of the production of the classic play Enemy of the People by Norwegian playwright Henrik Ibsen. I was stunned by the media bias as I read the article. It turns out that the play was revived recently by a theater company in Chicago right after the election of Donald Trump because the artistic director of Goodman Theater, Robert Falls, is no fan of the president.

NYT quotes Falls as saying, "I needed to do something about our sudden/current/soon-to-be ongoing horrific life under Trump and majority Republican rule," he said in an email.

Already the art director may have shot himself in the foot by taking on Donald J. Trump, a fact the NYT makes note of in the very next paragraph.

The NYT writes, "Little did he know that Trump would stamp the phrase "enemy of the people" in the American consciousness when he used it to pillory the news media in a tweet last February.

Donald J. Trump
✔ @realDonaldTrump

The FAKE NEWS media (failing @nytimes, @NBCNews, @ABC, @CBS, @CNN) is not my enemy, it is the enemy of the American People!

That's a fantastic tweet by the president by the way, and so true. My curiosity peaked, I went ahead and researched i.e. Googled the contents of the play that was brought back for the sole purpose of pillorying the president. When I found out what the play was about, I laughed out loud!

President Trump is supposed to be the modern "enemy of the people" but the original play written by Ibsen in 1882 is reminiscent of more recent events in Flint, Michigan. In fact, it's downright prophetic! The story centers on the main protagonist named Dr. Thomas Stockmann, a geologist who discovers that the water in his little resort town has become contaminated. He endeavors to use the local newspaper to tell the people about the contamination, but the newspaper, which is originally on board with the article, balks under pressure from the City Mayor Peter Stockmann, Dr. Stockmann's own brother.

The good doctor tries to go around the government and media obstacles in his path and takes his message straight to the people in a public meeting, but he presents himself in such a derisive elitist way that he ends of alienating his audience who brands him as the enemy of the people. His home is damaged, and he is practically run out of town. It's a real downer, but the message is clear, the hero cannot win on his own.

How this play would end up harming the president, I have no idea. It's like the theater people picked up a gun with a bad scope and ended up shooting themselves in the foot instead. Weird.

If you remember from recent news events and from my own blog, the real-life situation in Flint Michigan exactly mirrors the situation put forth in the play. Except that the contamination of the Flint water supply is not a natural disaster, but a man-made one brought on by the bad decision making of the city's leadership, lifelong democrats who attempted to hide the fact that their actions had dire consequences on their city. Indeed, the recent events there has inspired an adaptation of the play, called Public Enemy: Flint. I doubt the play mentions that democrats were to blame for the crisis and not our Republican president.

The Goodman Theater production has inspired theaters across the country to bring back productions of the play, including the Guthrie in the Twin Cities. Tickets became available in April and the play goes until early June. It would be interesting to see the play and gauge the reaction.

It's funny how artistic expression like live theater has an affect on matters in the real world. Art imitates life, imitating art. That brings me back to the play I saw that night. Newsies was based on a movie in 1992 that covered events in 1895 when young newspaper distributors, some as young as 9, organized a strike to protest unfair business practices of their employers, The New York World. Newspaper publisher Joseph Pulitzer, as well as other publishes jacked up the price that the Newsies had to pay for a batch of 100 papers. Originally the Newsies paid $0.50 per hundred, but Pulitzer jacked up the price to $0.60 per hundred. The Newsies were pissed and organized a city-wide strike. Apparently, the Spanish-American war had just ended and the buzz for the war had increased distribution of the paper, as well as revenue. With the war ending, the news cycle calmed down and circulation slacked off. The business leaders of the paper decided to recoup their losses by jacking up the prices on the little guy. It had the opposite effect.

Interestingly, when reports of what the Newsies were doing cropped up in newspapers, including the World, Pulitzer acted to suppress the stories in an effort to prevent the stories from damaging the paper's reputation. Interesting since Pulitzer was the very guy who founded the prestigious Pulitzer Prize for Journalism. A surprising nugget of information I did not learn in J-school!

In addition to suppressing the stories and blacklisting reporters who covered it, Pulitzer sends thugs with bats to break up the rallies organized by the Newsies. He sent men with bats to beat up children, let that fact sink in.

At the time of this strike, The World had been covering a railway strike that had been going on for months. What was good for the goose was not in this case good for the gander, at least where Joseph Pulitzer was concerned. I wonder if any recent Pulitzer Prize winners are aware of what a heal their hero was?

Interestingly enough the play casts Pulitzer as the villain he is but fails to mention that he was a lifelong democrat from the South who fought in the Civil War. So, I guess somethings don't change. The media, whether it is theater or the press or TV news, are great at focusing on content they want to cover, in order to vilify people they dislike, but are less willing to shine that light of truth onto themselves. It's interesting isn't it? But thanks to Google and Bing and the power of the Internet, the knowledge of the world is available at the touch of the fingers or even the sound of your own voice. It is important that in this modern media age that we don't get so focused on our own reality that we don't see what is happening outside our own little bubble.

Company towns and business leaders regardless of political stripe often take advantage of their workers in order to make a profit. It was true in 1800s New York and it's true for 2018 Rochester Minnesota. Leaders often cover up their mistakes while in an effort to make themselves took good while viciously assaulting their political rivals. The EPA, the Environmental Protection Agency under Barack Obama, caused a major contamination spill to ruin a river in Colorado, and has yet to make amends. Democrat leaders caused the Flint water crises. Has anyone heard about any of them going to jail? I could go on and on.

Plays like the one at Chanhassen and the Guthrie are fun nights of entertainment, and I'm not one to argue for the boycott of such plays. I suggest that the reader beware of any bias on behalf of the playwright and art directors when you attend. Sometimes you learn the truth in the enemy camp.

As for the actors and director of the Newsies produced at the Chanhassen, you are a talented crew and I thank you for an entertaining night out. We loved the pay and will come back again in the future. The serving staff was very helpful and gracious. The food was great and not too expensive.

If you book a seat for yourself and your crew, one word of advice. Get a table and avoid the booths in the far back. They suck.

6 FLINT TOWN

Officer Bridget Balasko drives her squad car up to the curb and parks. The sharp, crisp air of a Michigan winter greets her as she disembarks. She adjusts her gun belt and pulls her jacket collar about her neck to ward off the cold. She proceeds to walk to the door of the urban Flint home that was the source of the call. She is responding to a 911 call, 24-hours late.

It's a scene of the new docu-series on Netflix entitled Flint Town, and it is a winner. Abandoning the mundane techniques of storytelling so common with other reality shows touching law enforcement, this series tells a broader story of a dying metropolitan city through the lens of police perspective. Beautifully shot and directed, the candor of the police officers who participate is gripping and sad. A town caught up in poverty after a major car company left decades before, complicated by a water contamination crisis and a city government cover-up, there is tension in the air as events unfold. This is binge watch TV at it's finest.

A new mayor comes into power, promising change and a solution to the water crisis caused by the previous administration. Dr. Karen Weaver makes changes right away, firing the old police chief and hiring a new one. Together with the incoming chief of police, Timothy Johnson, the pair attempt to put their ailing city back together.

With only 98 officers covering an urban population of 100,000, Chief Johnson struggles to provide crime prevention coverage in a city where the average 911 call can garner a response in anywhere from 2-24 hours. Meanwhile the city council squabbles about how best to operate the city, making critical decisions about the budgets of the fire department and police department that are seriously undermanned and underfunded.

Filmmakers embedded with the police department for a year to provide 8 episodes, each less than an hour long and often not much more than 30 minutes long. It is easy to get caught up in the series and binge watch all 8 episodes in one day. This series is gritty and sad and I found watching that I was getting caught up with the stories of individual characters. I hope that the producers of this show produce a second series of 8 more episodes, longer this time, to let us know what happens to these courageous people in a story that is not well covered by the mainstream media. With the reaction of the police chief and the mayor on official channels, I find it unlikely, however, which is unfortunate. This is a true life story that needs to be told, and people need to watch.

The call that officer Balasko goes on does not go well. The African-American homeowner is not pleased that the police have been so tardy in responding to his burglary call. He blasts the young officer, who has been on the force only 3 years, and she listens with patience, taking in the details of the incident and a description of the men who robbed the homeowner. "I'm sorry it took so long to respond to your call," the officer says. "We've had a high volume of priority calls." Balasko apologizes again as she leaves the residence. She has 20 calls waiting on her overnight shift, and she has reports to write. She longs to be promoted to the detective bureau but because of changes in the department and budgetary shortfalls, her dream of becoming a detective has been put on hold. In the meantime, she struggles with the volume of work in an undermanned department where she often goes in alone to intimidating and dangerous situations. Balasko is only one of several dynamic real-world characters that if you watch you will want to get to know.

Whether or not there will be a follow-on series where we find those answers is up in the air.

Del Tackett (right) interviews Dr. Danny Faulkner, PhD, for the movie Is Genesis History

7 IS GENESIS HISTORY?

Blink and you might have missed it, but this week and last week there were limited showings of the new pro-creation vs. evolution film, Is Genesis History? staring Del Tackett, which appeared in theaters across the country. In this independent film, Tackett interviews PhD level scientists who hold a strong creationist view about their opinions of the Genesis Biblical account and how the physical earth evidence shows that the Global Flood appearing in the Bible could have happened.

Professionally shot with scenic locations around the world, Tackett creates a narrative, backed up by scientists, that Genesis is a historical account that can be backed up by physical evidence in geology, archaeology, astronomy, language, and history. It was enjoyable to watch the arguments, and anecdotally, in the second showing of the film I attended in Rochester Minnesota, the theater was packed with movie goers of all ages.

I liked it, and so did most of those who saw it. Rotten Tomatoes, who doesn't have any professional critique of the movie as yet, does say that 70 percent of movie goers who saw it report that they liked it. You can see some of the movie goer commentary here.

I've often felt that the theory of evolution and secular science instruction has killed the faith of a lot of young people attending high school and college. This movie seems to be an attempt at mitigating the damage and bringing young people back to faith. It does a good job with the arguments it makes. I can't wait until the show comes out in DVD so I can show my family and my church.

The movie is not without resistance though. Hard core atheists and the secular science community probably won't be jumping of their chairs and exclaiming, "you're right! We've got it all wrong!" But, this movie is a good beginning to the discussion for people who are on the fence.

Speaking of fence sitters: Bio Logos, a group of scientists who hold onto a Christian world view, but refuse to totally reject the theory of evolution, wrote a critique of the movie in the latest blog by Mike Beidler. Beidler argues that only two of the now well-known arguments are presented in the movie. A third world view, that which attempts a middle ground between the Bible's literal interpretation and evolutionary theory, is not included in the discussion and is totally dismissed. He says that those who study science don't have to reject either evolution instruction or their faith, there is a third way. He criticizes Tackett's film by not presenting a third world view in the body of the movie and talking deceptively and dismissively in a round table discussion following the movie. Beidler stops short of giving a blow by blow rebuttal of the evidence presented in the movie, but says that an understanding and acceptance of evolution doesn't need to endanger faith. You can read the entire blog at the Bio Logos website here.

There's apparently no love lost between the folks that made the Tackett movie and the folks over at Bio Logos. In a blog written a couple of years ago on the Answers In Genesis website, author John UpChurch states that Bio Logos is dangerous because they put people on a shaky middle ground that endangers their faith. The blog was written too early to comment on the Tackett move, but apparently the Bio Logos people and the Answers In Genesis people have a long history, and don't get along well. You can read UpChurch's blog post here.

While it is true that Tackett does not present this view in his movie, we don't think he should have to. After all, a Chevy dealer shouldn't be forced to give praise to the Ford company, do you think? Bio Logos seems well equipped to make their own arguments on their own platforms. It would be interesting to see people from the two groups debate, however.

I recommend this movie for parents, uncles and aunts, and grandparents to drag their millennial kids to see. It's not oppressive in it's presentation and it offers another look into different perspectives not seen in public schools and institutions today. It doesn't get to down in the weeds either, so the kids won't be rolling their eyes and falling asleep as they drown in scientific minutia. Overall I give this film an 8 out of 10. I look forward to seeing a DVD and other supporting materials coming out in the near future.

8 KELLI IN KUWAIT

For journalists and bloggers, access to government data and records can be a minefield filled with pitfalls. FOIA requests, documents, public meetings, interviews with politicians all have their challenges. How far would you go to get access to your government? Would you travel 5,000 miles to a combat zone and embed yourself in a military unit for a week? One local reporter did just that.

Kelli Lageson is the special projects editor at the Albert Lea Tribune and has been working for the newspaper for over two years. When two local National Guard units were mobilized to Fort McCoy prior to their deployment to Kuwait, Lageson was invited to cover a training event at the Wisconsin base. She happily accepted. During her visit with the units at Fort McCoy, it was discussed and Kelly agreed that she would look into embedding in the unit as a reporter and blogger once the unit arrived in Kuwait. She asked her bosses at Boone Newspapers, and the newspaper executives agreed to send her.

Lageson began working with the McCoy Public Affairs office and with two senior officers of the Minnesota Army National Guard, Major Paul Rickert and Lieutenant Colonel Kevin Olson. To her surprise it was relatively easy to fill out the paperwork necessary to become a credentialed reporter embed.

"They told me it was a possibility and I didn't really think it would be something I would be able to do," Lageson said.

Three months into the unit's tour of duty in Kuwait, Lageson arrived by commercial flight in Kuwait City. The scariest moment for her was waiting for the two soldiers to pick her up at the airport and take her to Camp Buehring, the remote desert Army outpost just 10 miles south of the Iraqi border.

"I didn't even have a phone number or a phone to call the soldiers who were picking me up," said Lageson. "I'm such a planner that I it was rather nerve-wracking for me. I just had to accept the fact that there was no plan and that I had to be O.K. with whatever happened."

The trip overseas and her journey through the desert were not without their pitfalls. She waited with expectation as the soldiers came to pick her up in a civilian car. Lageson, who says she liked to control and plan things out ahead of time, was worried that her escort, whom she had no control or contact, would arrive on time to pick her up. They did pick her up and they headed out to the desert as they promised.

Once they got to the base, however, the civilian security personnel did not allow her on base, skeptical of her memorandum and passport identifying her as a civilian journalist. After four hours of waiting by the main gain, however, a high ranking officer vouched for her and the journalist was allowed onto the base.

"One of the really high-ups had to come out and vouch for me and say, 'yes, she was a real journalist and she had a right to be here," Lageson explained.

Lageson reports that the overall experience with the unit was good. She was given an office to work out of, a reliable Internet connection, lodging and food. Her escort guided her around post and arranged for the interviews with soldiers that she asked for. While in Kuwait, Lageson gained access to soldiers from the unit and wrote 28 pieces with photos and video, she said. The soldiers, tentative about speaking with a reporter, warmed up to her eventually, she said.

Another item that surprised the reporter, was the amount of services provided to the soldiers, including a gym, recreational facilities, coffee shops, dining facilities, etc.

"I don't know what I expected," Lageson said. "It just wasn't that."

Lageson never left the base, it was too dangerous to go out with the units traveling north into Iraq. But she talked to a lot of soldiers and interviewed them about their daily lives. She says overall the trip was positive and the soldiers she met had a positive attitude about their mission, she said.

"The overal theme I guess I was trying to convey was that they were ok, at least on this deployment, that they were lucky to be on this deployment," she said. "Maybe that's a bad assumption but it was the overall impression that I had."

The response from readers of both the Albert Lea Tribune and Austin Daily Herald were positive too, Lageson said.

"Everyone wants to know, 'how is my son doing over there?' I got to show them a little bit of what life is like in Kuwait," Lageson said.

The military provided housing, food and an escort for the journalist while she was imbedded. She spent a week with Company D, 2nd Battalion 135th Infantry and a sister transportation company out of Austin. For her efforts in telling the stories of soldiers deployed to Kuwait, the soldiers awarded her a trefoil pin, an honor recognizing a soldier for doing a good job.

The distinctive crest of the 2nd Battalion, 135th Infantry Regiment, of which Co. D is a part. Note the trefoil in the center remembering the Civil War service and the phrase, "To the Last Man".

Historical note from the author. The First Minnesota Volunteers were noteworthy in the Civil War after being ordered to fill a breach in the Gettysburg lines. For five minutes they fought off an Alabama unit, outnumbered five to one. Of 262 members of the unit that reported that day, only 47 survived. Since that fateful day, the trefoil, the unit's distinctive patch, has been an honorary noting bravery in a soldier or a civilian attached to the unit. See a history of the First Minnesota Volunteers here.

Video, photos and print reports of Kelli's adventure to Kuwait is available on the Albert Lea Tribune and Austin Daily Herald websites under the blog Kelli in Kuwait.

See Kelli talk about her adventure in the video above.

Holly Hanson, R.N. with Haitian orphans.

9 HAITI RELIEF

In January of 2010, the island nation of Haiti suffered a devastating 7.0 magnitude earthquake that killed thousands and displaced many others. A year after the tragic event, the nation's citizens were still reeling from the aftermath where disease, homelessness and poverty were rampant.

Leaders of the Mayo Clinic in Rochester, after an extensive safety evaluation, decided that it was safe enough for teams from the clinic to travel to Haiti and provide medical support. Gordon Griffith, R.N., and emergency department nurse, was one of those selected for the mission and served on the second of ten teams that traveled to Haiti to provide medical support.

Griffith arrived in Port Au Prince where Mayo Clinic Team 2, under the leadership of Dr. Chris Farmer, a pulmonologist, embedded itself with a charitable organization already on the ground, Operation Blessing. The mission of Team 2 was to provide medical services to a hospital and clinic run by Dr. Rick Frechette, a Catholic Priest, medical doctor and missionary.

You can see Fr. Frechette's early commentary about the earthquake's effects on You Tube here.

Griffith and other members of the team were impressed by Frechette even though they worked with him only a short time, Griffith says.

"He's a catholic priest, who is also a doctor, who givers sermons in combat boots," said Griffith, describing Frechette. "He was an amazing man and quite inspirational to hear."

Team 2 stayed and provided assistance for just one week, providing education and medical care to patients in poverty. Cholera was one of the major diseases common amongst the patients seen by the team, a result of the deplorable sanitary conditions of the shanty towns in which many of the population lives, Griffith said.

About midway through Team 2's week of service, the team was allowed to visit an orphanage for young children displaced by the earthquake. Many of the children are without parents because of the earthquake or were abandoned because of severe injury or illness. According to Griffith, the purpose of the visit was just to provide comfort to the children who have little affection or human contact.

"We were allowed to see one of the orphanages that Operation Blessing had organized," Griffith said. "It was developing into an oasis. We got to interact with all these kids, and because they no longer had their parents, many just had an innate need to be held and so we as care givers just gave."

"They (the children) indicated what they needed," continued Griffith. "And for a while we were able to provide some time for that." The clinic was clean, well-organized and had a competent, caring staff which provided many healthy activities, food and clothing for the children under their care, Griffith said.

One of the major goals of the teams sent by the Mayo Clinic was to provide care at a level that was sustainable by the Haitians themselves after the teams of healthcare workers were gone, Griffith said.

Holly Hanson, R.N. of the Mayo Clinic Team 2 documented the trip with her photography, some of which we include here. Hanson also produced a You Tube video describing the teams mission here.

Frechette's charitable work earned him recognition in the United States and he was awarded the Hollywood Humanitarian Award in October of 2009.

Hollywood Actress Maria Bello, of the hit TV series ER, made the award presentation to Frechette.

"We were there (in Haiti) to visit Father Rick Frechette and his life-changing programs for the poor," says Bello. "(He) is a priest and doctor who has lived and worked in the slums of Port Au Prince for decades. He saw the conditions of the poor and disenfranchised, and works tirelessly every day to bring dignity and hope to the people there."

Accepting the award, Frechette said,

"It is a sign of your interest to help the poor children of Haiti to move to a world of more Justice, more peace and more opportunity."

Describing the charisma of the humble priest, Griffith said.

"He is a man equally comfortable addressing the rich and famous, politicians and movie stars, as he is talking and working with humanitarians and the poor disenfranchised children of his parish."

Mayo Clinic Team 2 consisted of the following members: Dr. Chris

Farmer, Dr. Mark Enzler, Dr. John Meuller, Gordon Griffith R.N., Shannon Hackbart R.N., Shannon Rodriguez R.N., Amy Brabec R.N., Holly Hanson R.N., Kathy Asp R.N. C.N.P., Laurie Vlasak R.N. C.N.P.

Disclusure: Gordon B. Griffith is the older brother of the author of this column. He has served previously as a Peace Corps volunteer for two years in Guatemala, Central America; has served as a Navy Corpsman providing medical relief as part of a Navy Fleet Hospital in Togo West Africa; and provided medical support as a Corpsman to a detachment of U.S Marines in the early days of Operation Iraqi Freedom. He works as an emergency department nurse at Rochester's Mayo Clinic.

Members of Mayo Clinic Team 2, in Haiti.

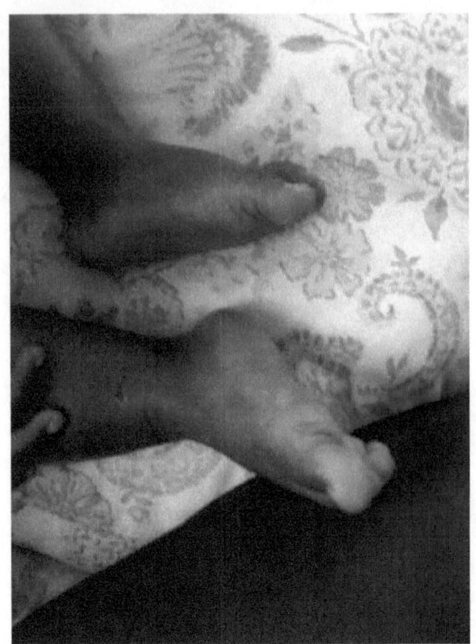

A child's Feet. -photo by Holly Hanson, R.N.

Gordon Griffith R.N. of Mayo Clinic Team 2 with an orphan child in Haiti -photo by Holly Hanson, R.N.

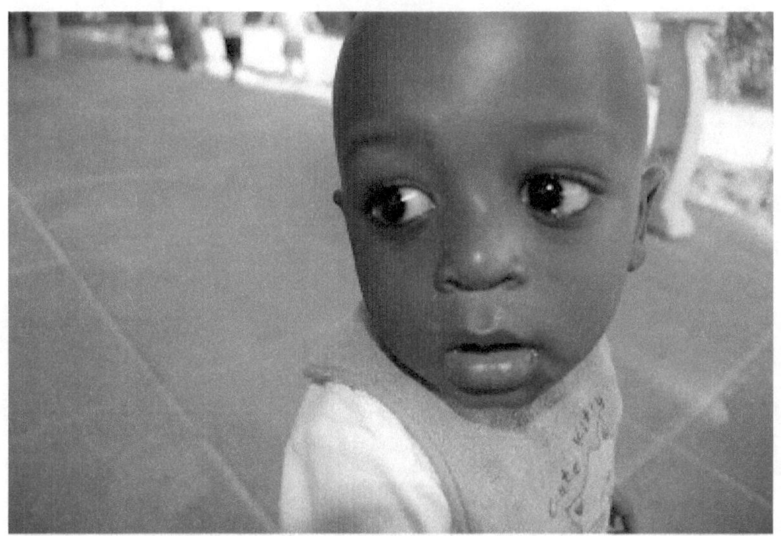

(Gordon Griffith, R.N. of Mayo Clinic Team 2 talks about his trip to provide medical support to the devastated community of Haiti following the earthquake there. A longer, more detailed version of his comments can be found here.)

Children are encouraged to draw what they see at Art in the Hollow Event Saturday. Performers, artists and musicians gathered at the Swede Hollow Park to participate in a daylong event. - photo by Jeremy Griffith

10 ART IN THE PARK

Performers, artists, musicians and craftsmen gathered at historic Swede Hollow Park in St. Paul Saturday to show their stuff. Onlookers came to circulate amongst the performers to listen and to see what the craftsmen had for sale.

This year's lineup included the Mariachi Estrella, a premier Latin and Spanish musical group, Aztec performers from the Kalpulli Yaocentoxtli Mexican/Aztec Dance and Drum Group, and a children's group from Mounds Park American Indian Magnet School, amongst others. For a full list see the website at Artinthehollow.org.

St. Paul, (June 2, 2012) Harpist uses Swede tunnel as a megaphone to capture the attention of passersby during the 2012 Art in the Hollow event. Artists and musicians gathered to show off their talents Saturday. - photo by Jeremy Griffith

St. Paul, (June 2, 2012) Kalpulli Yaocenoxtlix Traditional Aztec Dancers demonstrate at Swede Hollow Park during Art in the Hollow Day. The dancers were part of a number of artists and musicians who participated in daylong event. - photo by Jeremy Griffith

St. Paul, (June 2, 2012) Mariachi Estrella band plays Latin, Mexican Regional and Spanish Pop music at Art in the Hollow day at Swede Park Saturday. Performers, dancers and artists participated in a daylong event. -photo by Jeremy Griffith.

St. Paul, (June 2,2012) Artists capture the scene at Art in the Hollow event at historic Swede Hollow Park Saturday. - photo by Jeremy Griffith

11 ROSELLE IS MY HERO

You know it really irritates me that Chelsea Clinton finds herself this week on the cover of Variety Magazine as one of the women power players of New York. I mean, come one, what are her accomplishments, other than being the silver-spoon fed brat of Hillary and Bill Clinton?

A photo recreation of the Variety cover featuring Chelsea Clinton. I've replaced Clinton's face with the face of my wife to represent who the real hero should be.

And, her patronage by Bill is even an open question.

Other than being the daughter of two really big power players in the democrat party, Chelsea has literally no street-cred of her own. And yet, the media fawn over her relentlessly. I haven't even read the Variety article. The cover of Chelsea alone makes me want to vomit.

Instead I wanted to write a feature of my own, covering one of my personal female heroes: my wife, Roselle Salvador Taburada Griffith.

Roselle came to the United States from the Philippines about eight or nine years ago by invitation of her first husband, who will remain nameless. That marriage was doomed from the start and Roselle struggled to establish herself as productive American citizen on her own. With the help of family and friends, Roselle got her green card and got her first job, at Target of all places, as a cashier. From then she got a better paying job as a food service worker in a major hospital in Minnesota.

Roselle came from a lower middle-income family in Tacaroung City on the southernmost island of Mindanao Philippines. They didn't have much, but all of the kids, seven I think, got college degrees. Roselle got a business degree before coming to the United States. She works hard and plays hard. For a past time she joined the prestigious Park Institute of Tae Kwon Do and the tutelage of Grand Master Kun Yu Park and an associate instructor, Mr. Peterson, a former Marine. She attained her First Dan in Tae Kwon Do within four years and competed all over the US and Canada, winning several medals and trophies. (First Dan, by the way is a black belt for those of you who don't know.) One of her fellow sparring partners is on a major competition circuit and herself has won many awards.

She met yours truly later on and I was smitten. I helped her transition from green card holder to naturalized citizen. Getting her citizenship papers and being sworn in was one of the proudest moments of our lives. Because of her studying, she can quote details about American History better than most people who were born here. In a brief moment of lapse in judgement, she agreed to marry me, and made me the luckiest guy in the world.

Recently she got her picture hung on the wall at work, having been named the Employee of the Month. That's because she shows up on time, works hard, cares about her job, and offers absolutely no slack.

This past weekend, she proved again that she can hang with the boys by proving her metal with a shot gun. We attended an Easter weekend party and a bunch of us tried our hand at skeet shooting. She smoked me, as well of most of us, men and women. It was her first time shooting the 12-guage shotgun. At the end of the day she had a bruise on her arm and a smile on her face.

These all might not be grandiose accomplishments to you. But, they mean a lot to us. We are not rich, famous, powerful; we are just normal people, which is why I'm writing this article. Variety Magazine, along with much of the mainstream media, is so out of touch with the rest of the country. They raise up people of no accomplishment but plenty of celebrity while ignoring the rest of mainstream American. Roselle and people like her work hard and earn everything they have, which isn't much. People like Chelsea Clinton whatever her married name is have their lives handed them on a silver platter.

Roselle is the epitome of what a naturalized citizen should look like, which is why she will never be interviewed by a major media outlet or magazine like Variety. She doesn't fit the narrative. Stupid girl, instead of just jumping the border, she followed the law, and emigrated here legally. Instead of stealing benefits and welfare funds from taxpayers, she became a taxpayer and works hard for every cent. And at her earliest opportunity, she took the plunge, paid her fees, studied for oral and written exams and became a naturalized United States Citizen.

Out of touch, elitist magazines like Variety are just self-licking ice cream cones of the left. They're like Hollywood award shows, the actors and directors self-congratulate, and nobody watches. This is why Donald Trump won the Presidency of the United States, by the way. It's because the left and right coasts are so out in left field, trapped in their little bubble-boy echo chamber that they don't see that the America they once dominated is slipping away from them. Good.

12 STAR TREK DISCOVERY LAUNCHES

Star Trek Discovery for what it is worth has had an OK start in its two first episodes of the first season. Time will tell if the series is worth paying $6 for monthly streaming access.

Set in an era 50 years before the era of James T. Kirk and Mr. Spock, Bones McCoy, Chief Scott and all the rest, it is a turbulent era where the rules of the United Federation of Planets is not quite set in stone. Being the latest of the Star Trek endeavors, the technology and feel of the series looks to the future rather than the past. That is because there is no putting the genie back in the bottle. Times have changed, and technology has changed with it. Do you really want to go back to those trite early scripts and laughable sets of the 1960s?

The new series introduces us to a number of great characters, gets us to like and identify with them a little, then starts messing with our heads. For me it was like reading We Were Soldiers Once and Young for the first time, when the author introduces us to likeable characters and then kills them off. Too obscure a reference, Game of Thrones then. A likeable captain Philippa Georgiou is killed off in episode two, oh, spoiler alert, and her first officer Michael Burnham is sentenced to life in prison.

Oh, but magically she gets whisked off to the USS Discovery where she is employed by the controversial Captain Gabriel Lorca, where presumably the series kicks off into high gear. I love Jason Isaacs as an actor and he is evidentially going to play Lorca. I'm totally stoked for this fact. I have great hope for this series, I've been a big fan of Star Trek all my life and I want to go on watching the series and am emotionally invested in it.

Having said that, the cast has not shied away from controversy on the political spectrum and it's necessary to talk about in this blog. Amidst the controversy of American sports professionals taking a knee at games while the National Anthem is played, the Discovery crew decided to take a photo of them taking a knee as well. It makes sense from a certain perspective. Star Trek has always been about diversity, and actors who sign up for series like this are well aware of the complexities of race relations in this country, which are very very bad. All of us who grew up watching the series know the political history of the show. Actress Nichelle Nichols, an African American, had a prominent role in the first series and was thinking of leaving, but stayed on because noted Civil Rights leader Martin Luther King Jr. asked her to stay on as a role model for others. Since then, the cast and crew have always shown us that diversity is an important factor in a great and adventurous future.

That being said, I'm ok for now that the cast took a knee. Too me, they are protesting the horrible treatment of African Americans in this country, which continues to be bad. But in my mind it is different than when sports heroes do it in the midst of the National Anthem. The National Anthem and our flag represents all that is good about America and what we aspire to be, not unlike the dream of the Federation, it represents the hope that a diverse people can be great in achieving common goals. By kneeling during the Anthem, to me it is like we are burning our national symbol and with it our hopes for shared achievement and diversity. I can't see the flag disrespected any more than I could the principles of a United Federation.

I'll give the crew of Discovery the benefit of the doubt for now. But the real issue seems to be not just solidarity with oppressed peoples, but with a firm hatred for Donald Trump and what he represents. This I'm sort of baffled by as well, but you can see it in the national media and in the way many people in Hollywood treat our president. Ten years ago you wouldn't know that Trump was a racist. He helped minorities out and he got recognition from current civil rights leaders for what he achieved for African-Americans. Immediately after putting an R behind his name and running for president, trouncing a horribly lackluster candidate, Hillary Clinton, suddenly The Donald is Adolf Hitler. That is a hugely unfair characterization in my estimation. So far there is no genocide of brown people, there is no destruction of the US economy, the economy is doing better if anyone bothers to look at the numbers, and the status quo seems to be maintained such as it is.

Some might feel that Trump is unnecessarily jingoistic in his responses to Iran and North Korea, but it is previous administrations that have put us in this situation, not The Donald. It was Barack Obama who gave billions of our tax dollars in cash to a rogue state that wants nothing less than the annihilation of the Israeli state, followed by the destruction of the big Satan, America. It was previous democrat administrations that gave a green light to North Korea to develop nuclear strength, and it is the reason the mighty midget is now threatening his neighbors and us with nuclear destruction. The Donald is not trying to start a war, he is trying to deal with Kim Jung Un and the mullahs of Iran in the only language that they understand, force!

I have an analogy that the crew of Discovery and Star Trek fans will be sure to appreciate. In the first two episodes of Discovery, Michael Burnham and her captain are faced with an incredibly violent and war-like adversary, the Klingons. The Klingons only understand one thing, war. It is their code and creed. Captain Georgiou, like all Star Fleet captains, wants to be an explorer, not a warrior. They see the risk, but instead of preparing a defense, they try a stance of appeasement. Of course, as predicted, that goes horribly wrong, it sends the wrong message to the enemy and it launches Star Fleet in a horribly destructive war that will cost many lives. If they had listened to Burnham, and given the Klingons the "Vulcan Hello", things would have worked out quite a bit differently.

Now it is up to Lorca, a captain who doesn't quite follow the rules, to deal with the Klingons, ultimately defeat them or fight them to a draw, so that the Federation can eventually get back their original goal and mission, peaceful exploration of space and interaction to the wonderful and strange new worlds and people therein.

Now here is where the analogy meets reality, and I doubt that liberals in Hollywood will like it, but they ought to hear it from a fan. Donald Trump is Captain Gabriel Lorca and Michael Burnham is his Secretary of Defense, Gen. Mathis. Ouch. Really? Yes really. The appeasers playing Captain Georgiou, bless her heart, Hillary Clinton, Barack Obama, Bill Clinton, take your pick of the weak spine democrat in office. They created a horrible mess with an enemy that cannot be reasoned with and now the Donald, aka Lorca has to roll up his sleeves and get down to business before the Klingons, aka North Korea and Iran nuke us all to death.

It's kind of like when Jean-Luc Picard went up against the Borg. We thought everyone was going to die, but one guy with the guts to stick his neck out was able to win the day, at very great cost. Picard is Trump. Someone should remind Whoopie Goldberg of The View of her Star Trek roots. Her character Guinan was a popular character on the The Next Generation series and was an able advisor to Picard. I would love to hear her take on this blog. She hates Trump.

Sucks but there it is. You are welcome, Hollywood.

As I have said, I love the Star Trek series, and I have high hopes that this series will carry on the noble tradition. I'm sure they have some great stories to tell. We will see if they deliver on their promises.

For Further reading, check out what Jason Isaac has to say about his new role, his castmates and "taking a knee" here.

https://www.yahoo.com/entertainment/star-trek-discovery-postmortem-jason-isaacs-fan-theories-taking-knee-013012506.html

Abu Tahseen, stalking ISIS in the Iraqi desert with a homemade weapon that looks like a Star Wars prop. The Silver Sniper, 63, was killed in Northern Iraq this week fighting terrorists.

13 TALE OF TWO SNIPERS

A 63-year old veteran sniper has died in the service of his country, drawing interesting parallels between another sniper who in a single act of incomprehensible rage killed 59 of his fellow countrymen at an outdoor concert in Las Vegas. This is a tale of two snipers.

His name was Abu Tahseen, and he's not a household name here in the United States, but he should be. He was known by his various nicknames: The Silver Sniper, the Sheik of Snipers, and Hawkeye. A veteran of five wars over many decades, the man was feared by his enemies, and his enemies, the latest ones, were the dreaded fighters of ISIS who ran rampages across Iraq and the Middle East causing fear and suffering wherever they went. Tahseen was not afraid of them and indeed, is credited with killing 341 of the vile terrorist, blasting them into oblivion with his bolt-action .50-caliber BMB sniper rifle. Tahseen is on record in video bragging that when his bullets struck their mark, the victim would be blasted backwards a meter or more by the sheer force of the impacting round.

Now ISIS has made a mess of the Middle East, has threatened everyone who doesn't adhere to their extreme ideology, but The Silver Sniper, a devout Muslim, was not intimidated and was dedicated to destroying them, one at a time. On average, he is said to have sent four of those vile murders to their maker every day, and no one was safe within a mile of his rifle.

Sadly this hero has passed away, martyred in one last battle to free his country in the battle for the northern Iraqi city of Hawija. Terrorists have claimed credit for taking Tahseen down, but a blind monkey sometimes finds a banana in the jungle on occasion. Hopefully, others will rise to the occasion and fill the gap that Tahseen has left.

Songs should be sung of this hero. A blockbuster movie needs to be made, with a novelized tie-in. I look forward to that. In the meantime, read Taryn Tarrant-Cornish's great article in Express *here,* and find out more about this remarkable man who stalked the desert with a homemade weapon that looked like it was a prop for the latest Star Wars movie.

Here in the United States the 24/7 news cycle knows nearly nothing about this great man, but is preoccupied with another gunman, I hesitate to call him a sniper, Stephan Paddock, 64. Paddock as you may have heard, occupied a hotel room on the 32nd floor of the Mandalay Hotel in Las Vegas and using several weapons modified to shoot near-fully automatic, rained deadly bullets onto unsuspecting concertgoers below. No motive has been found on why this wealthy gambler who made his money in real estate would do this horrible thing. He is not brave, or noble. He was a coward and died a coward's death. When rough men armed with guns came to stop his horrible onslaught, he turned his gun on himself rather than be captured or killed by men braver than himself.

What is interesting about these two men, as different as night is from day, is their shared similarities. Both are senior citizens, both are known for what they did with a gun. But there the similarities end. Tahseen was a hero. At 63, when he should have been enjoying retirement, he went to the aid of his country, like Cincinnatus of Rome, he served when his country called and died the hero.

Paddock meanwhile had the kind of life many in this country only dream. He worked as a postal worker, an accountant, he worked for the IRS at one point, and he made his money in real estate. His father was a famous bank robber who at one point was on the FBI's most wanted list, which might explain this man's mental disconnect. He was a fixture at the hotels and casinos, spending large sums of cash at the tables. Then, inexplicably, this crazy decided he had had enough of the good life and without any other obvious motive, destroyed the lives of 59 innocent people and wounded over 500 more. Political and media pundits blame the guns and lax gun laws for this man's actions, but we ask that we look at the man, not the tool.

Let's compare and contrast these two men for a moment. Tahseen, a veteran with decades of experience, was a skilled rifleman. With his bolt-action .50 BMG he killed 341 people, animals really, in defense of his nation. Paddock tried to do as much, only his victims didn't deserve it, had no idea it was coming, and were like fish in a barrel in his senseless onslaught, unable to shoot back or defend themselves in any way. We can see that in the hands of two very different men, a gun, a tool, can have very different results.

We recommend that Muslims, indeed anyone who admires skill and bravery, carve the name of Abu Tahseen on concrete and stonewalls in memorial of his bravery and achievements to liberate his countryman. For Paddock, list him on an historical footnote, and then immediately forget him, but don't you dare forget his innocent victims!

FROM THE WRITER OF AMERICAN SNIPER
THANK YOU FOR YOUR SERVICE
INSPIRED BY TRUE EVENTS
OCTOBER 27
A UNIVERSAL RELEASE

14 THANK YOU FOR YOUR SERVICE

The movie "Thank You For Your Service" was more than a movie for me, it was a deeply moving experience that everyone should watch, especially if you have a loved one who served in the Global War on Terror.

I was in Iraq, for 15 months. I often feel like I was a well-armed, well-trained, well-payed tourist. My logistics job didn't allow me to go out on patrols every day, though I would very much have wanted to. My brigade was in Iraq for so long because we were extended for the surge. We had more consecutive days in combat than any other unit, so I get it. Having said that, I never saw anyone die, and I never fired a shot; my job did not require it.

When I heard about this movie, of course I wanted to see it. I hoped that it was not some cheesy make a buck off the war movie that got everything wrong. I hoped there would be action. It was not that kind of a film. Instead the story centered on one squad of soldiers and their squad leader on one or two days fighting in Iraq. Staff Sergeant Adam Schumann is on patrol in his convoy in a bustling city somewhere in central Iraq. This is about 2007-time frame, the same time I was there. The patrol goes terribly wrong, and there are casualties.

The movie fast-forwards to the soldiers' arrival at their home base of Fort Riley, Kansas. From the combat patches worn by the soldiers, it can be guessed that they belong to the Big Red One, 1st Infantry Division. The soldiers are greeted by loved ones as they get off the plane, and then they attempt to re-integrate back into their regular lives. This story is poignant and sad as the soldiers fight their own battles at home, often alone without support. It is extremely aggravating to watch. Bring tissues, or just do what

I did and wipe your nose on your spouse's sleeve. What is especially maddening is that when the soldiers find that they do need help, they are often offered only roadblocks in the form of uncaring leadership, administrative buffoons, pride, laziness, greed, etc. One side note. I worked with many people who work for the VA, who care deeply about soldiers and want to help. So what I am about to say is not for them. Close your ears. If you are working for the VA and you don't care about soldiers, only your big fat salary and benefits then you can go find a job somewhere else. Heroes need to help heroes. You don't have to have been a soldier, but you do have to care about your patients. Go find some other government cubicle to hide in.

This movie dramatically shows for the viewer the kind of internal struggle many of our soldiers go through, and when I say soldier, I mean everyone who has served, Airmen, Marines, Sailors, Coasties, everybody. Suicide, mental illness, drug and alcohol addiction, paranoia, grief and survivor's guilt, it all hits you in the gut with this movie. I won't ruin the plot further, just go see it, and be prepared to cry.

But it isn't enough to just go to a movie and have a good cry. This movie is a call to action. Based on the book of the same name by Pulitzer Prize winner David Finkel, it is the directing debut of Jason Hall. Brilliant acting by lead actors Miles Teller as Schumann and Haley Bennett as his loving wife Saskia. Comedian Amy Schumer has a dramatic supporting role as a grieving widow. Good job to all. Their storytelling is more than just entertainment, they do great service for soldiers who have seen action and are now struggling.

As I said before, it isn't enough to watch a movie and cry, this show is a call to action. The VA failures are not just the failures of big government bureaucracy; it is the failure of us all because we don't care enough to fix it. When is the last time you've called up the VA and asked them for a report on how they are serving the soldier? When have you called your local representative? If the answer is no, I have to ask why not? What is stopping you? Do it tomorrow, won't you? See this movie tomorrow and then go call someone and get them to see it.

Traumatic stress disorder is no joke. We've been at this global war for 16 years, and there is no sigh of let up. We lost four special operators in Niger last week. I wonder if mainstream America will ever come to realize that the problem of global terrorism is not going away and that the problem with the VA and with soldier mental and physical health is not going away. Would you want your children to suffer?

I can't say enough about this movie, but I have to wrap up. Rotten Tomatoes gives this movie a giant golden tomato, which is good for them. We agree for once. I guess a blind monkey can find a banana in the jungle, because they are often wrong. Good for them for getting it right for once.

15 THE END OF MILO?

I actually am very sad and I almost don't know what to write. Is this the end for controversial Alt Right media personality Milo Yiannopolis, or can he go on from here?

Milo is a gay British man living in the United States who has been a free speech advocate and has been until recently the editor-in-chief of Brietbart News. He did have a lucrative book deal pending as well, but all of that came crashing down when Milo made some seemingly inappropriate comments on a video interview about pedophilia. And while I haven't watched the videos myself, I understand from others who have that the content is seriously disturbing.

In the aftermath of these comments, Milo has come under intense pressure and has resigned his post at Breitbart. The publisher with whom he was negotiating his book deal has withdrawn from publishing the book. Yesterday, Milo apologized, but also vowed to go on, speaking at campuses about free speech and continuing with his own media company. We wish him the best.

But we cannot agree with what he has said. Pedophilia is not ok and children should be allowed to grow up in a healthy, safe environment free from any kind of pressure of an intimate nature. Such pressure exerted at an early age by an adult is assault and it is shameful. We have sympathy for Milo as a victim of child rape himself, but we don't excuse his actions or his words.

Dana Loesch on her TV show on The Blaze made a lengthy comment about this and we would like to echo those comments. While we understand that the left will use this circumstance to destroy Milo, and that is not ok either, we cannot support his comments either and there must be a price for such thoughtlessness. Maybe Milo is paying that price now.

But is Milo continuing to be a victim here? Can you be a victim and a victimizer at the same time? We believe so and while we don't want to cut Milo off completely, it may be necessary to take a cooling off period. The upcoming CPAC, where Milo was scheduled to speak this Friday has said as much and has disinvited him from that speaking engagement. We feel this is the right move under the circumstances.

Is it right to say anything you want? While it is allowable under our First Amendment, it isn't always wise, and while we have a right to say what we feel and think, there is often a cost to doing so. You can't just tell your boss to F off without expecting the subsequent and inevitable termination. You can't hit a cop and not expect to be dragged off to jail. You can't tell jokes about sex with minors and not expect to lose a few friends. Milo is finding that out today.

In light of any difficult situation, as Christians we are called to be our higher selves, even while we don't feel like it. I feel that if Jesus Christ were here, he would roundly condemn the sin, but he would also love the sinner. We ought to follow Christ's example, love the sinner, hate the sin, and leave the judgements to God. When Peter condemned his neighbor Matthew, the bloodsucking, worthless tax collector, Jesus said in reply, "Well, do you think he would invite us for supper?"

That's how it should be with us. One of my favorite passages in the Bible is when a disciple of Christ is asked to drop what he is doing and go evangelize a transgender political figure passing through the town. The disciple hastens to the road where the eunuch is passing by on cart. The fellow is reading a scroll containing the scriptures. That provides an opportunity. "Do you understand what you are reading, there?!" the disciple asks. "How can I?" they reply, "Unless someone explains it to me."

The disciple is invited up into the carriage and he explains the scriptures to the eunuch, who later asks to be baptized. This is a great story that should be repeated in the present day, but sadly isn't. We as Christians often act more like Pharisees ready to stone the prostitute; not at all like the disciple on the road who explains the scriptures to a transgender seeker. And meanwhile, Jesus is waiting in the wings and drawing in the dirt, waiting for us to do the right thing and do what he told us to do.

The author and his wife travel to Vegas a month after the terrible shooting that killed 58 innocent concert goers.

16 THE SHOOTER IS TO BLAME

The City of Las Vegas and the whole United States is reeling today three days after the horrible shooting in which 58 people died and over 500 were injured. As investigators try to piece together why this happened politicians are quick to jump to the default conclusion to blame the gun and not the idiot with the gun.

Hours after the shooting was reported, former presidential candidate and Secretary of State Hillary Clinton tweeted her support for increased gun control legislation. The evening comedians likewise jumped on the band wagon to call for something, anything to be done and vilifying anyone who would oppose it.

But really, what, if anything, can more gun laws do to prevent something like this from happening in the future. As has been pointed out previously, terrorists who want to cause destruction have wreaked havoc without using a gun. Timothy LaVeigh comes to mind, who used a box truck and fertilizer to kill hundreds.

Early reports say that the shooter used two bump fire stocks on his gun that convert semi-auto weapons into firing full auto. There is speculation that that device will now be under scrutiny for banning in the future due to the damage it caused. Reason Magazine published a great article yesterday describing what a bump fire stock looks like and how it functions. You can look at the full article here, including a video demonstration.

Jacob Sullum of Reason explains that the bump stock seems to sacrifice accuracy for speed, vastly increasing the number of bullets sprayed from the gun. It makes the gun hard to control and is considered a novelty used by gun enthusiasts rather than really increasing the lethality of the firearm.

Sullum writes, *"Assuming that (Stephan) Paddock (the shooter) used the bump* *stocks police found, did they make the number of deaths higher than it otherwise would have been? Not necessarily, since bump stocks sacrifice accuracy for speed; the jostling required by the technique makes the rifle harder to aim, especially at long distances. According to the Wikipedia entry on bump stocks, they "greatly degrade the accuracy of the firearm, due to the necessary jerking of the weapon, which makes viable aiming impossible," and "the inaccuracy renders the practice uncommon."*

Sullum eloquently points out that other shootings that did not use this feature have proven extremely deadly as well, while not as deadly as the Las Vegas shooting. But in Vegas, the lethality was most likely aided by the shooters tactical position on the 32nd floor rather than any accessory he may have used.

At the end of the day, this tragedy was caused by a madman with an axe to grind. An evil heart made this happen, not an inanimate object. Those guns didn't jump off the shelves into this man's hands. He methodically planned this atrocity, collecting guns and ammo over a long period of time. He reconned his target and chose his firing position with care. This coward was perfectly fine with killing innocent people who were unable to fight back, but when a fire team of officers can knocking on his door, he decided to check out rather than face them.

So instead of blaming the gun, we should blame the idiot. And then we should forget him. We should all be ready to help the victims and their families as they deal with the tragedy. It will be a long time before they get back to a sense of normalcy, indeed, they may never fully be the same. Americans should not be punished by a reduction of their rights because of the evil acts of one idiot

17 THE NATURE OF GOD

Here are some thoughts that occurred to me the other day as I was waiting at the post office. It was a rather long line and I had a lot of time to think. My thoughts revolved around the nature of God.

Let's assume for argument sake that God does exist. There is plenty of evidence from nature that he does in fact exist, but I won't go into those in this column. So, let's just start with the assumption.

With that as our starting point, we ask the question, what is the nature of God?

Have you ever had that overbearing relative, the parent, brother, or brother-in-law? You go to family reunions, after you've grown up, and no matter how old or experienced you get, you always have that relative or several of them that are always digging on you, telling you how to live your life, diminishing your capacity, encroaching on your freedom to choose. They always give you unsolicited advice, and after you've rolled your eyes for the fifth time, they still go on and on, espousing their philosophy about how you should go forward? "Buy a house! Get out of debt! Get married! Get a better job! Why are you doing that? Don't you care about your future?" And on and on. It gets annoying, doesn't it? If you have the capacity, maybe you run away out of town, or maybe even out of state to avoid the constant lectures. That way, you only have to deal with the unsolicited behavior from Uncle Mike on holiday get togethers. Then it doesn't get too oppressive and is easier to deal with.

I think a lot of people think that God is that way. His rules are too oppressive, restrictive. If you believe in God then you have to follow his rules and that isn't any fun. You want to live your life and stretch your wings, find your own sense of fulfillment. You don't want God looking over your shoulder, like some obscene sky ogre messing everything up. A lot of people I think have this view. There's a scene in the cult classic series Firefly with main characters Preacher Book and the pirate captain Malcolm Reynolds. Book says something to the effect of, "Everyone loves a preacher!" to which Reynolds says, "No they don't! Preachers make you feel guilty and judged!" Exactly.

A lot of people are resentful of God and his rules because they resent that relative that is always trying to run their lives. They say that the image of God in people's minds is driven by their opinion they have of their father and I think to some extent that is true.

But God is not like that. He is quite different. He's very much like a parent though and he does set down some rules for us when we are young, to keep us safe. He establishes these rules as guild lines so that we more or less follow them in adult hood as a way to live happy lives and keep us out of trouble. A parent establishes bed times and meal times, curfews for teen agers. They establish rules about when we go back in and what time we have to be home. But the rules are always changing, especially as we evolve from children into grownups. We get more and more freedom to choose for ourselves what we will do, and I think God does the same for us. The basic principles are always there, they just evolve as we get older and more mature. The basic tenants of His law are always with us: don't kill, don't steal, don't lie about a neighbor, don't be jealous of your neighbor's stuff. That never changes. But God doesn't continually nag at you about what you are doing in your day to day life. He isn't nagging you about taking that job, or investing in a certain way, or marrying the right girl. In other words, he's not like your aunt Milly. Like him, you have free will to choose what you do with your life, within the rules He has set for you. He has established the rules as guidelines for a happy life. Follow them, and you will be happy. Ignore them and you will have to pay the costs. God doesn't enforce the penalties; the penalties exist all by themselves.

Cheat on your wife, for example, and she will find out. Good luck with that. Three years into the divorce, when you are mad at the ex about custody rules she's enforced on the kids, and you want them on a certain weekend, a weekend that happens to be hers, reflect on the fact that it's your own fault that you are here. You declined to follow the rules. Now pay the consequences.

If you embezzle money from your boss, you will eventually get caught. Go ahead and explain to the judge that the rules didn't apply to you. See how that works out. You'll be in a small room with bars right across from Bernie Madoff.

Some say the rich and famous don't pay the same penalties that you would, but they do. In spades. Ever read about celebrity divorces? They are ugly and expensive. Neglected spouses get millions in payouts from their cheater partners and so forth. Politicians are the same way. Look at Anthony Weiner. No don't, on second thought. He's gross. But you see what I mean. How about Bill Cosby and OJ Simpson? Sure, their trials came out in their favor, but eventually the consequences do catch up, and it pays a terrible toll. Nobody gets over the consequences.

So really, following the rules God has laid out, only leads to a happier life. Someone explained it to me this way. Have you ever played a game with someone who doesn't follow the rules? You hit a shot in, and they call it out. You're playing the new board game and the rules always seem to come down in their favor? That sucks and eventually you stop playing with them because it's no longer fun anymore. That's what life is like outside the rules. Eventually, it's no longer fun.

Finally I think the ultimate consequence of a rebellious life is a Hell we create for ourselves. I don't think God throws people into Hell so much as they throw themselves into their own version of Hell. Just like I don't think Lucifer is any kind of a lord of the afterlife. I think he and his angel followers will be banished to a far corner of the universe apart from the warmth of God's love where they will be forever engaged in a never ending battle of King of the Hill. Everyone scratching and clawing for the brief moment on top. And all of us sinners who reject God will be tossed in with them, for eternal misery. I think of it this way. God is the sun. You bask in his light forever like sunbathers on the beach, surrounded by nice people. Or you can be exiled to the darkest cave of the arctic, left to fend for yourself, surrounded by people who hate each other.

That's it, that's my theory about the nature of God. As you can see. It was a very long line at the post office that day, and I had a lot of time to think. What do you think? Leave your comments down below.

18 THROUGH THE RED DOOR

So I was invited to do some exploration of the Minneapolis area recently by a close, close friend who was curious about finding out more about a socialist/communist enclave there. Apparently, where he lives he is seeing people with Russian Spetznaz tattoos and his curiosity was piqued. So was mine and I agreed to take a look.

It should be noted that this friend lives far, far from the Minneapolis area, so I was invited to investigate. He didn't know much. All he knew was there was a communist bookstore in town and around a corner was a tattoo place where people indulged in getting the Spetznaz tattoos. Spetznaz are the Russian version of special forces operators and getting the tattoos I guess is a sign of support for anything communist or socialist. I don't know why anyone who hasn't served would want a military tattoo, let alone a special forces tattoo. If I suddenly decided to sport a SEAL tattoo, I think Karma would serve me and a real Navy operator would find out and kick my ass, and I would deserve the beating. While I didn't find evidence for the tattoos, I did find a book store or two that met the description of the starting point of where I was looking.

Apparently over on Cedar Avenue not far from the University of Minnesota campus there is a bookstore in the basement of a business complex that sells communist literature and propaganda. It's called May Day books, presumably for the First of May celebration of the birth of Communism in Soviet Russia. They have a parade every year. On street level at that building there are a number of businesses that rich hippy kids going to school would love to browse, an expensive bike store and a Mountaineering gear supply store complete with a climbing wall training area. All of the businesses on the main floor are connected and you can walk from one to the other. Except for the bookstore. That you had to access through a side exterior staircase that led into a dingy basement. A huge painted logo on the side of the building with yellow paint and bold letters announces progressive books are sold below.

Following down where the arrows point, you find the stair case with a bright red railing leading you down. At the bottom of the stairs is a red door, as red as can be, and through the door is May Day books. I felt like Alice in Wonderland falling through the rabbit hole. I opened the door and stepped inside. I would not have been surprised to see the Mad Hatter.

It's a quaint little shop with shelves on every wall. It contains only one room and very well could be the meeting place for a failed Hillary Clinton campaign headquarters in that area. At the front door to the right is a rack of communist and socialist literature, most of it not terribly current. The election of Donald Trump has taken a bit of the wind out of young progressive sails, apparently, and nobody has the energy to write anything fresh. I started to browse. A store keeper was nowhere to be seen.

I normally love book stores and I have to say, while I would probably not purchase a lot of what the store had to offer, the titles and subject matter intrigued me. Here was a bastion of liberal and progressive thought, ground zero for the enemy's propaganda and information operations campaign. This was it and I wanted to dive in and see what the left was saying about my beloved capitalist system and free markets.

A sign above the counter announced that the store hadn't made a profit since its establishment in 1975, the year it was established. Not something most businesses would care to brag about. I started to look around. There was a lot of anti-capitalist tomes available and one even had the title, or something close to it, "Capitalism sucks and here are 10 top reasons why!"

I found one or two books that would be fascinating reading, no matter the content. One was, "Bible stories for the Atheist" and there was another on a female Palestinian hero who fought against alleged Israeli aggression. There was a lot of anti-Semitic propaganda books, a little on so-called Islamaphobia. There was a lot on the Vietnam war and some on the most recent wars in Iraq and Afghanistan. Most of these decried the evils of American Imperialism squashing ancient Middle Eastern cultures to steal oil, or something like that. Any one of these stories would have been an interesting read. There was a whole wall of shelves committed to Malcom X. Interesting.

A store keeper came in eventually from a cave at the back of the store, greeting us politely. He was an older man with a crooked, painful looking twisted leg. He had me pegged as an old soldier at once, there was no hiding from him, even though I'd started to grow my hair longer. He was a communist, not an idiot. He asked me if I'd been in the service and I said yes. He informed me that he had been at Hue (pronounced Way, Vietnamese, I know right?) He asked me about what I thought about the current situation in Syria. I was non-committal, avoiding displaying my true feelings and talking about Trump.

"I think it's a powder keg and it has always been a powder keg," I said, and I left it at that. On the way out of the store the guy behind the counter gave me a leaflet on a veterans for peace organization. I accepted it politely and left. I was proud of myself that I actually made it out of a bookstore without buying a book. That rarely happens.

My wife and I went upstairs and looked at bikes and canoes, many too expensive for me to afford right now. I appreciated the irony. Maybe I miss my guess, but the guy's rent in the basement doesn't pay for the building, the budding capitalists upstairs more than provide for rent and jobs and revenue for the whole block. There were some nice items there for young rich kids to buy with their monthly allotment from their wealthy parents. There was even a climbing wall in the mountaineering portion. Very cool. My hands sweated just thinking about it. I am not much of a climber.

We left that establishment and found another communist museum to a failed ideology. Boneshaker Books in the Seward neighborhood was our next destination. True to its reputation, they had a lot of books not often found in other places. They got me for about $40 for only two books. There was an Asian gentleman around the counter managing the place, and a young Caucasian woman eating some organic dish right in the middle of the store largely ignoring my wife and I. It's a good thing we found the place because we hadn't stopped all day and my wife and I both had to use the bathroom. (One of the bathrooms at the store was down, but the one we saw that still functioned was clean and well-kept.) It was either that or the laundromat down the street which my little Asian wife patently refused to use.

Boneshaker Books is a little bigger than May Day and has a tiny collection of rare books and art. On the door is a sign decrying their need to love diversity, being good liberals that they are, that read: "We embrace our Muslim brothers and sisters. All are welcome! Stop Islamaphobia!" I wonder if the bookseller would be as welcoming if they knew I was a diehard conservative with libertarian leanings? My wife and I didn't fail to notice that there were definitely Somali and Muslim influences in the neighborhood. We entered a grey stucco building covered with elaborate vines and we were not disappointed. I put several books back on the shelves not for wanting to have them, but just to preserve my hard-earned cash. I have too many books as it is.

Off one corridor was a conference room where it appears they had meetings where young liberals talked about whatever young liberals talk about. I didn't see a sign for the Hillary Clinton Election Failure support group, but I didn't look that hard. I imagine some of that is going on. To one side close to the entrance I saw a rack of propaganda almost exactly like the one at May Day. Apparently, they're on the same distribution list. I didn't take anything this time. On the walls above the books were several drawings by local artists for sale, many of them very nicely done. One thing liberals often do better than we conservatives is art, literature, and poetry. They're wired that way and they are very good story-tellers. Unfortunately, much of the stories they tell are fantasy fiction. It doesn't work in real life. But, looking at the art and pursuing the books, I couldn't help being impressed. I put several books back which I would normally have been very interested in, like history, war, insurgency and that sort of thing. There was a copy of 1984 and Upton Sinclair's Jungle, which I thought was interesting. (All of these young kids should actually read 1984 rather than just stock it on shelves, but I digress.)

I actually picked up two titles that I hadn't heard of before. One was a graphic novel called "Pride of Baghdad" by Brian Vaughan and Niko Henrichon. It's the story based loosely on a true event that happened in Baghdad during the 2003 invasion to oust Saddam Hussein. Apparently, we bombed a zoo, the lions got out, and we shot the lions. End of story. I didn't care much for the dialogue, but the art of the panels and the premise of the story were intriguing. I give it a 7 on a scale of 1-10.

The other one I picked up was called, "Narco-Economics, How to Run a Drug Cartel" by Tom Wainwright. I think it will make an interesting read and will go along with my binge TV watching of Breaking Bad on Netflix. In my mind, I think it will provide some information for research I'm doing on another story line I'm working on. Wait and see. It's written by a guy who apparently has done journalistic work for The Economist in their Mexico City office, as well as for the Guardian, the Times and Literary review. I'll let you know how it is.

I made my purchases at the counter and the store keeper offered us free buttons. "Fuck Trump" they said. That's why they were free, nobody would take them. My wife and I politely declined and left the building.

The next stop on our journey was a little shop around the corner, at Tattoo establishment. A tall thin man with ink and piercings came out from the other room. I think we largely wasted our his time, for which I apologize. It was evident to him from the beginning we weren't interested in getting tattoos, we didn't seem the type. I was much more interested in seeing if he had any evidence that that was the store where the Spetznaz tattoos came from. I asked a couple of questions about art and pricing, which he politely indulged, and then we left him to his real customers. I was impressed with the artwork that he had on display. If the actual tattoos look anything like the art displayed on the walls, then the workers really know their business.

The rest of the day my wife and I spent shopping at Asian groceries in Minneapolis and St. Paul. My wife is Filipino and once a month I indulger her in her quest for seafood. There are a couple of nice shops that are usually well stocked, but this time were not. Must be a bad time of the year for sea fish? We visited Shaung Hur off of University Avenue which had nothing, so we migrated to the store of the same name off of Nicolette. There we actually did get some fish and shrimp, which made my wife extremely happy. My wife pointed out a weird looking fruit she likes called Durian. It looks like a big, green, spiky alien head. I imagined that if you cut it open, an alien baby would pop out and eat your head like in the classic horror movie, Aliens. They make a Durian drink like a milk shake that is actually a very sweat, white frothy concoction with a green aftertaste. My wife and I stopped around the corner to try one at a little Vietnamese kitchen. Then we went over to a Mexican restaurant next door and had lunch. It was expensive, but the food was good. I had a Cerveza Dos Eqius, which is uncharacteristic for me. I usually don't drink beer in the middle of the day.

At the end of the day, I was struck by the oddity and contrast of our little mission to Minneapolis. So many contradictions. Communists decry the horror and unfairness of capitalism, but all around them capitalism thrives, the mountain bike store, the Mexican and Vietnamese restaurants, the Filipino and Asian food stores, all of them thrive because of free markets. Even the communist and socialist books stores thrive from the free market place of ideas. Some would say that their goal is to shut down the debate of competing ideas. I am a free speech guy. Let them try to spread their failed ideology. They can forever be a case study in the museum of wrong thinking. I agree with Sean Connery who said in a movie once that we should be reading books rather than burning them. How else do we challenge our closely held beliefs?

The communists didn't win me over, and I didn't win over any of them. But I had a good time exploring enemy territory.

For further reading:

http://www.citypages.com/arts/top-7-bookstores-in-the-twin-cities-6576379

https://www.theguardian.com/world/2003/apr/22/iraq1

http://www.boneshakerbooks.com/

http://maydaybookstore.org/

19 TOWN HALL

Congressman Tim Walz-D, CD1 of Minnesota, looking dapper and hip in blue jeans, brown leather shoes, white button-down shirt and blue blazer, met with constituents in a rare town hall meeting on Thursday in the Rochester Community and Technical College's Charles E. Hill Theater.

It was rare because Walz, who won back his seat in the House of Representatives by the narrowest of margins last election cycle, rarely meets with the regular public, only donors. But this was different and the glib and professional looking Walz helped himself greatly in the effort.

There were a lot of issues discussed at the town hall, which was packed to standing room only at the edges where Walz made a brief statement in the beginning before answering questions from the audience non-stop for two and half hours. The subject matter of the town hall ranged widely from the disputed fate of the failing Affordable Health Care Act, to National Security and Immigration. But there was one big take away.

Walz will not rule out a run for the Governorship of Minnesota.

A lady in the crowd asked the Congressman if he would run, eliciting his response. Many of the crowd showed their opposition of such a move, preferring him to remain in his current position. Still, there was a lot of applause as well when the Congressman said he would not rule it out. That applause may be indicative that a win for Walz in a governor's race is at least possible.

Governor Mark Dayton, the incumbent, will be through with his latest term in two years and is not expected to run again. Dayton has been struggling with cancer and had a scary moment at his latest State of the State address when he passed out briefly at the end of his speech.

Running for Governor instead of his old seat in the congress may be a good move for Walz considering the slim victory he had over Republican challenger Jim Hagedorn the last time. Hagedorn is an able campaigner and has run against the incumbent twice before. With the unpopularity of the ACA and Walz's liberal stances in a largely conservative district, three times might be the charm for Hagedorn. Conversely, Walz might make a much better showing in the statewide race especially factoring in blue areas including the Twin Cities Metro area, Rochester, Duluth and the Iron Range areas.

While Walz has said he won't rule out such a campaign, he has not acknowledged a desire to run and it isn't a sure thing. We'll just have to see.

Meanwhile, in the two and a half hours Walz spoke to constituents, several things became clear:

1. There is a lot of concern about ACA and medical coverage in general and the ACA has failed to meet the expectations of the voters in meeting its promises of lowering costs, increasing coverage, and increasing or maintaining choice. Indeed the opposite is true for many, which the congressman freely acknowledged.

2. People are concerned about immigration, especially of refugees from areas of concern named in the travel ban enacted by the Trump administration and challenged in the courts. Walz acknowledged those fears saying that national security concerns are a real issue, but stopped short thereafter, saying that it was wrong to demonize an entire sector of people, namely Muslims, who worship differently and have different cultural practices.

3. Walz would like the public to believe that health care is a journey and not a destination. He says he would like to see an ACA fix rather than an out and out repeal. Indeed he joked about a repeal and replace that came back on November 9, after an election cycle where it can do little damage to politicians struggling to win in elections, a common tactic used several times by the Obama administration. Many don't think this is a terribly funny joke as their health care insurance provided in part by their employers have been cancelled and not replaced. Many others feel tied to their jobs when other opportunities avail themselves, because the coverage at a new employer may not be as good as what they have in their current job. Still many others have not gotten insurance, despite tax penalties, because they are healthy and don't have jobs that will allow them to afford the coverage and high deductibles.

4. People are concerned about their privacy considering the knowledge that the government has the technology to spy on their telephonic conversations and internet usage. One attendee commented to the congressman that while privacy is important, the idea that a sitting National Security Advisor having his private phone conversations listened to and

recorded shows the nation's enemies what our capabilities are. NS Advisor Lieutenant General Michael Flynn was recently allowed to resign his new post after it became clear that he was having phone conversations with Russia prior to the election.

One question that seemed to take the discussion on a completely different tangent was the concern of one attendee who was against the so-called militarization of police forces. He son was on the local police force and was a current member of a SWAT or tactical team. Walz allowed that seeing officers in heavy gear and uparmored vehicles created a tension between cops and the community, but also said he favored legislation that provided equipment for local officers to be well protected in the execution of their very dangerous and hazardous duties of protecting the public.

In Walz's appearance Thursday, he seemed to be very adept at playing both sides against the middle. Nothing he said in the meeting seemed to be outrageously right or left. If you're a national security guy, you might be lead to believe that Walz is as worried as you. But then he denounces efforts by the Trump administration in carrying out his duties as commander in chief by temporarily banning refugees from Muslim minority countries of concern also black listed under the Obama administration. If you were for the ACA, you might believe that Walz is for improving it and are worried that Republicans will throw it in the trash. If you thing the ACA is a failure, you might get a sense that Walz is actually for a fix that might actually just be repeal and replace.

In essence, Walz was soft on specifics when it came to individual policy decisions that he would support or oppose, only indicating that he didn't want to "diminish anyone's concerns".

When asked if he supported the continued federal funding of abortion provider Planned Parenthood, for example, Walz simply said "yes" and left it at that. There was no discussion of how Walz felt about the realization that P&P was actually selling the body parts of aborted fetuses for profit to medical research companies and whether or not he felt that practices was wrong and the practitioners prosecuted.

If you were looking for a kill stroke that showed Walz as a radical leftist as his voting record seems to indicate, you didn't see it in this public appearance. What you did see is the slow acknowledgement that the Obama administration's chief accomplishment, the ACA, is not living up to expectations and desperately needs to be fixed, repealed or replaced. Walz's support of the law is likely the chief reason he nearly lost the last election round and why he should probably seek another office where his chances are better.

Watch a video of highlights of the town hall meeting below.

20 VOTER ID LAW

Minnesotans will soon have to choose whether or not to require photo ID at the polls. The state legislature placed a constitutional ballot amendment question on November's ballot after Governor Mark Dayton vetoed a voter ID bill last year.

The amendment question is a yes or no question asking voters whether or not they want the constitution of Minnesota to require voters to present valid state photo ID when they vote. Proponents say the bill will cut down on willful voter fraud in the future, while opponents say it will disenfranchise certain voters who are unable to get photo ID, such as shut ins, nursing home residents, and overseas residents.

Recent polls indicate most Minnesotans favor a voter ID law.

Rep. Mike Benson, a primary architect of the bill, says it will empower voters because so much of what we do on a day to day basis requires an ID and points out that those seeking government services require a photo ID in any case.

"Voter fraud is so difficult to detect and it is cost prohibitive to prosecute," said Benson. "It's not a priority for local county attorneys with the other crimes they have to deal with. This measure will help to detect potential voter fraud before it happens."

http://www.youtube.com/watch?v=-ZFX5n5jVvA

Rep. Mike Benson comments on Voter ID Constitutional Amendment Question. Video by Jeremy Griffith

Sen. Carla Nelson explained that voters who show up to the polls can still vote through a provisional ballot system. The bill will do away with vouching, but will not eliminate same day registration, she said.

"This bill, let's be clear, will do away with the practice of vouching," said Nelson. "It will not eliminate election day registration. And those who cannot afford photo ID, the government will provide one for them."

http://www.youtube.com/watch?v=qoduhQNGfrE

Sen. Carla Nelson Comments on Voter ID Constitutional Amendment Question. Video by Jeremy Griffith

Dan McGraff, executive director of Minnesota Majority, had a lot of input into how the bill was presented to the legislature. His organization found irregularities after the heavily contested election of 2008. According to statistics he found from the State Secretary of State's office, over 23,000 postal verification cards sent to verify the new same day voter registrations came back because they were unable to find a valid address or a person at the address that met with the description of the person registered. Since the 2008 election over 400 people have been identified as having voted illegally and 113 have been convicted, he said.

The 2008 election was the year when Al Franken-DFL narrowly defeated incumbent Republican Norm Coleman for the US Senate seat. The Minneapolis Star Tribune, with statistics from the Minnesota Canvassing Board, shows how close the election was before and after legal challenges and a six week recount process.

Opponents of the ballot question say that voter fraud is actually well below one percent of the 2.9 million who voted in the 2008 election, and that the amendment would further disenfranchise voters who would otherwise not be able to get a valid photo ID.

According to the National Conference of State Legislatures, there are currently over 30 states that have some kind of voter ID law on the books today.

You can hear debate for and against the proposed amendment at the Minnesota State Legislature's website here.

BIBLIOGRAPHY

1 INTRODUCTION

2 STEALING JOY

Griffith, J. L. (2018, July 25). Stealing Joy: The Dark Side of the Fair. Retrieved from http://www.americanmillenniumonline.com/stealing-joy-the-dark-side-of-the-fair/

3 COWARDS OF THE COUNTY

Griffith, J. L. (2018, February 24). All Four Deputies Arriving at Broward County School Shooting Failed to Enter School. Retrieved from http://www.americanmillenniumonline.com/all-four-deputies-arriving-at-broward-county-school-shooting-failed-to-enter-school/

4 DARKNESS DAVE

Griffith, J. L. (2012, August 02). Darkness Radio. Retrieved from http://www.americanmillenniumonline.com/darkness-radio/

Griffith, J. L. (2012, August 06). Darkness Dave Schrader Video Interview (Update). Retrieved from http://www.americanmillenniumonline.com/darkness-dave-schrader-video-interview-update/

5 ENEMY OF THE PEOPLE

Griffith, J. L. (2018, May 09). Media Bias Backfire: An Attack On the President in Live Theater Could Be a Shot to the Foot! Retrieved from http://www.americanmillenniumonline.com/media-bias-backfire-an-attack-on-the-president-in-live-theater-could-be-a-shot-to-the-foot/

BIBLIOGRAHPY CONTINUED

6 FLINT TOWN

Griffith, J. L. (2018, March 25). "Flint Town" Netflix Docuseries Explores Dark Side of a Dying City. Retrieved from http://www.americanmillenniumonline.com/flint-town-netflix-docuseries-explores-dark-side-of-a-dying-city/

7 IS GENESIS HISTORY?

Griffith, J. L. (2017, March 08). Is Genesis History? Movie Review. Retrieved from http://www.americanmillenniumonline.com/is-genesis-history-movie-review/

8 KELLI IN KUWAIT

Griffith, J. L. (2013, February 27). Kelli In Kuwait – An Adventure of an Embedded Journalist. Retrieved from http://www.americanmillenniumonline.com/kelli-in-kuwait-an-adventure-of-an-embedded-journalist/

9 HAITI RELIEF

Griffith, J. L. (2012, August 12). Mayo Clinic Employee Remembers Service to Earthquake-Ravaged Haiti. Retrieved from http://www.americanmillenniumonline.com/mayo-clinic-employee-remembers-service-to-earthquake-ravaged-haiti/

10 ART IN THE PARK

Griffith, J. L. (2012, June 16). Performers, Artists and Musicians Gather at 2012 Art in the Hollow Event. Retrieved from http://www.americanmillenniumonline.com/performers-artists-and-musicians-gather-at-2012-art-in-the-hollow-event/

11 ROSELLE IS MY HERO

BIBLIOGRAHPY CONTINUED

12 STAR TREK DISCOVERY

Griffith, J. L. (2017, October 02). Star Trek Discovery Launch is a Go! Retrieved from http://www.americanmillenniumonline.com/star-trek-discovery-launch-is-a-go/

13 TALE OF TWO SNIPERS

Griffith L. (2017, October 11). The Tale of Two Snipers. Retrieved from http://www.americanmillenniumonline.com/the-tale-of-two-snipers/

14 THANK YOU FOR YOUR SERVICE

Griffith, J. L. (2017, October 29). Thank You For Your Service Movie was a deeply emotional experience! Retrieved from http://www.americanmillenniumonline.com/thank-you-for-your-service-movie-was-a-deeply-emotional-experience/

15 THE END OF MILO?

16 THE SHOOTER IS TO BLAME

Griffith, J. L. (2017, October 04). Blame the Idiot, not the Gun! Retrieved from http://www.americanmillenniumonline.com/blame-the-idiot-not-the-gun/

17 THE NATURE OF GOD

Griffith, J. L. (2017, July 09). A Brief Explanation of the Nature of God. Retrieved from http://www.americanmillenniumonline.com/a-brief-explanation-of-the-nature-of-god/

BIBLIOGRAHPY CONTINUED

18 THROUGH THE RED DOOR

Griffith, J. L. (2017, April 12). Through the Red Door: My weekend journey to explore communist bookstores and tattoo shops in Minneapolis. Retrieved from http://www.americanmillenniumonline.com/through-the-red-door-my-weekend-journey-to-explore-communist-bookstores-and-tattoo-shops-in-minneapolis/

19 TOWN HALL

Griffith, J. L. (2017, February 27). Crowds Pack College Theater as Congressman Tim Walz Makes Rare Town Hall Appearance. Retrieved from http://www.americanmillenniumonline.com/crowds-pack-college-theater-as-congressman-tim-walz-makes-rare-town-hall-appearance/

20 VOTER ID LAW

Griffith, J. L. (2012, June 17). Minnesotans Will Decide Voter ID Question in November Election. Retrieved from http://www.americanmillenniumonline.com/minnesotans-will-decide-on-voter-id-requirement-in-upcoming-november-election-ballot-question/

Griffith, J. L. (2013, February 27). Minnesota Voters Struggle over Fate of Voter ID Constitutional Amendment. Retrieved from http://www.americanmillenniumonline.com/minnesota-voters-struggle-over-fate-of-voter-id-constitutional-amendment/

ABOUT THE AUTHOR

Jeremy Griffith is the creator of the American Millennium Online blog. He is trained as a journalist and has served in the military, including a long tour of duty in Iraq. He is married and lives in Rochester, Minnesota with his family.

OTHER BOOKS BY JEREMY GRIFFITH AVAILABLE
AT AMAZON.COM.

DANCE INTO FIRE

THE HOUSE ON SPIRIT LAKE

LSA ADDER: THE LOGISTICIANS